THE DEATH OF CAESAR

Borgo Press Books by VOLTAIRE

The Death of Caesar
Saul and David
Socrates

THE DEATH OF CAESAR

A PLAY IN THREE ACTS

VOLTAIRE

Translated and Adapted by Frank J. Morlock

THE BORGO PRESS

MMXI

THE DEATH OF CAESAR

DEDICATION

For my son, Miles Morlock

CONTENTS

CAST OF CHARACTERS

JULIUS CAESAR, Dictator

MARK ANTHONY, Consul

JUNIUS BRUTUS, Praetor

CASSIUS, Senator

CIMBER, Senator

DECIMUS, Senator

DOLABELLA, Senator

CASCA, Senator

CINNA, Senator

ROMANS

LICTORS

ACT I

The action takes place at Rome in the Capitol.

ANTHONY:

Caesar, you are going to reign; behold the august day
In which the Roman people, always unjust to you,
Changed by your virtues, is going to meet in you
Its conqueror, its support, its avenger, and its king.
You know, Anthony cannot envy it;
More than you I have cherished the glory of your life;
I've prepared the chain you are putting the Romans in,
Satisfied to be under you, the second of mankind,
Prouder to attach this new diadem to you,
Prouder of serving you than reigning myself.
What! You don't reply to me except by long sighs!
Your grandeur is my joy, and displeases you!
King of Rome, and the world, is it for you to complain?
Can Caesar tremble, or can Caesar fear?
Who can inspire terror in your great soul?

CAESAR:

Friendship, dear Anthony; it makes my heart open to
  you.
You know that I am leaving you, and that destiny
  directs me
To carry our standards to the fields of Babylon.
I am leaving and going to avenge on the inhuman
  Parthians
The shame of Crassus and the Roman people.
The eagle of the legions, that I still retain
Demands to fly towards the seas of Bosphorus;
And my brave soldiers are only waiting for the signal
So as to see my face again belted with the royal crown.
Possibly, Caesar can rightfully undertake
To attack a country that submitted to Alexander:
Perhaps the Gauls, Pompey, and the Romans
Subjugated by my hands are worth more than the
  Persians.
At least, I dare think so; and your friend flatters
  himself
That the conqueror of the Rhine can be conqueror of
  the Euphrates.
But this hope that animates me doesn't blind me;
Fate may tire of marching at my heels;
The greatest sagacity is often deceived.
Having betrayed Pompey it can leave Caesar.
And in factions, as in battles,
Triumph or defeat is only a step apart.
I have served, commanded, conquered, for forty

years;
I've seen the destiny of the world in my hands.
And I've always known that at each event
The destiny of states depends on a moment.
Whatever may occur, my heart has nothing to fear.
I will concur without pride or die without self pity.
But, in sharing your tender friendship, I demand
That Anthony and my children be forever linked.
That Rome, by my hands, defended and conquered,
That the earth to my sons, as to you, be submissive;
And that bearing away from here the great title of king
My blood and my friend will take it after me.
I am leaving you today, my last will;
Anthony, my children must be served like their father.
I don't wish to demand any oaths of you,
As sacred but vain guarantees of human faith;
Your promise suffices, and I think it more pure
Than the altars of gods surrounded by perjurers.

ANTHONY:

It's already a harsh enough law for Anthony
That you are seeking war and death without me.
And that your interest attaches me to Italy
When glory is calling you to the shores of Asia.
I am more afflicted still to see that your great heart
Doubts its fortune and suspects a mishap;
But I don't understand your goodness which outrages
    me,

Caesar, when you tell me of your son, of sharing?
You have no son except Octavius, and on no adoption
Has another Caesar to support your house.

CAESAR:

There's no time, friend, to hide the bitterness
Which secretly is consuming my fatherly heart.
Octavius is my blood, only by favor of the law.
I've named him Caesar, he's the son of my choice:
Destiny (ought I to call it propitious or harsh)
Has made me indeed father of a true son.
Of a son that I cherish, but who, to my misfortune
Responds with horror to my tender friendship.

ANTHONY:

And whose is this child? What ingrate can be
So unworthy of the blood that the gods caused him to
    be born of?

CAESAR:

Listen: you know the unfortunate Brutus
In whom Cato cultivated the rough virtues.
That austere defender of our ancient laws,
That rigid enemy of arbitrary power

Who, always against me, arms in hand,
Followed the fate of all my enemies;
Who was my prisoner in the fields of Thessaly,
Whose life I saved twice,
Born, nourished far from me at the home of my
    proudest enemies—

ANTHONY:

Brutus! He could be—

CAESAR:

You don't believe it; here, read this.

ANTHONY:

Gods! Cato's sister, the proud Servilia!

CAESAR:

She was joined to me by a secret marriage.
That proud Cato, in our first struggles,
Almost before my eyes made her pass into other arms.
But the day that established this second marriage
With her new spouse decided destiny.

Under the name of Brutus my son was raised.
Was he reserved, O heaven, to hate me?
But read, you will know everything from this funereal
    writing.

ANTHONY:

"Caesar, I'm going to die. The celestial wrath
Is going to end my life and my love at the same time.
Remember that Caesar gave life to Brutus.
Goodbye. May this son prove to his father
The friendship that his mother retained for you as she
    was dying!
Servilia!"

What! Must the tyrannical law of fate,
Give you a son that so little resembles you, Caesar?

CAESAR:

He has other virtues; his superb courage
Secretly flatters mine, even when he outrages it.
He irritates me, he pleases me; his independent heart
Assumes a proud ascent over my astonished senses.
His firmness impresses me, and I even excuse him
For condemning supreme power in me;
So that being man and father, a seductive charm
Excuses him in my eyes and deceives me in his favor;

So that being a Roman, the voice of my country
Speaks to me despite myself against my tyranny,
And that the liberty that I've just oppressed
Even more strongly than I, condemns me to love him.
Shall I tell you even more? If Brutus owes me being,
If he is the son of Caesar, he must hate a master.
I thought like him from my earliest years.
I detested Sulla, I hated tyrants.
I would have been a citizen if proud Pompey
Hadn't wanted to oppress me under his usurped glory.
Born proud, ambitious but born to be virtuous,
If I weren't Caesar, I would have been Brutus.
Every man to his situation must bend his courage
Brutus will soon take a different tone,
When he shall know of what blood he is born.
Believe me, the diadem is destined for his face.
It will soften his importunate roughness,
He will change his manners as he changes his fortune.
Nature, blood, my blessings, your advice,
Duty, interest, all will make him my son.

ANTHONY:

I doubt it, I know his fierce fortitude:
The sect he belongs to doesn't allow anything to move
    him.
This intractable sect, which boasts
Of hardening spirits against humanity.
Which tames and crushes under its feet irritated

nature,
Alone speaks to Brutus and alone is heard.
These frightful prejudices, that they call duty
Have an absolute power over their bronze hearts.
Even Cato, Cato that unfortunate stoic,
That wild hero, the victim of Utica
Who, fleeing a pardon that humiliated him,
Even preferred death to your kind friendship.
Cato was less lofty, less harsh, and less to be feared
Than the ingrate that your bounty is attempting to
    constrain to love you.

CAESAR:

Dear friend, with what blows have you just struck me?
What are you telling me?

ANTHONY:

I love you and I cannot deceive you.

CAESAR:

Time softens all.

ANTHONY:

My heart despairs of it

CAESAR:

What! His hate—

ANTHONY:

Believe me.

CAESAR:

Never mind, I'm his father.
I've cherished, I've saved my greatest enemies.
I intend to make myself loved by Rome and by my
    son;
And conquering vanquished hearts through my clem-
    ency
To see the earth and Brutus adore my power.
It's up to you to assist me in such great plans;
You've loaned me your arm to subdue men;
Subdue Brutus today, soften his courage,
Prepare this virtuous savage by degrees
For the important secret that must be revealed to him
And about which my heart still hesitates to tell him.

(Enter Dolabella.)

DOLABELLA:

Caesar, the Senators are awaiting audience.
They've come here at your supreme order.

CAESAR:

They're slow enough. Let them come in.

ANTHONY:

Here they are.
What scorn and hate I read on their faces.

(Enter Brutus, Cassius, Cimber, Decimus, Cinna, and Casca, with lictors.)

CAESAR: seated)

Come, worthy supports of Roman grandeur,
Companions of Caesar. Come forward, Cassius,
Cimber, Cinna, Decimus, and you, my dear Brutus,
Finally, here is the time, if heaven seconds me,

In which I am going to complete the conquest of the
    world
And see the throne of Cyrus in the Orient
Fall, to satisfy the manes of Crassus.
It's time to add, by right of war,
That which is lacking to Romans of the three-quarters
    of the world.
Everything is ready; all foreseen for this vast design.
The Euphrates is awaiting Caesar, and I am leaving
    tomorrow.
Brutus and Cassius will follow me into Asia.
Anthony will retain Gaul and Italy.
From the Atlantic Ocean to the shores of Betis,
Cimber will govern subject kings.
I am giving Greece and Lycia to Marcellus,
Pontus to Decimus, Syria to Casca.
Having thus regulated the fate of nations,
By leaving Rome happy and without divisions,
It only remains for the Senate to decide under what
    title
I must be the arbiter of Rome and mankind.
Sulla was honored by the name of dictator,
Marius was Consul, and Pompey emperor.
I conquered this last and that's enough to tell you
That we need a new name for a new empire.
A name greater, holier, less subject to reversals,
Formerly feared in Rome and dear to the universe,
A rumor much confirmed spreads over the earth
That it is in vain Rome dares to make war on Persians
That a king alone can vanquish them and give them

the law.
Caesar's going to undertake it and Caesar isn't king.
He's only a citizen known for his services
Who can still dry up the caprices of the people. . . .
Romans, you hear me, you know my hope.
Think of my benefactions, think of my power.

CIMBER:

Caesar, I must speak. These scepters, these crowns,
This fruit of our toil, the universe that you are giving,
Will be, to the eyes of the people and the jealous
    Senate,
An outrage to the State: more than a benefit to us.
Marius, nor Sulla, nor Carbo, nor Pompey,
In their authority over the usurped people,
Have ever pretended to dispose at their will of
The conquests of Rome, and to speak to us as kings.
Caesar, we were expecting from your august clem-
    ency
A gift more precious, a favor more just,
Above the States given by your bounty.

CAESAR:

What are you daring to demand, Cimber?

CIMBER:

Liberty.

CASSIUS:

You promised it to us, and you yourself swore
To forever abolish absolute authority:
And I was thinking to reach at this happy moment
When the conqueror of the world was going to fulfill
    our wishes.
Smoking in its blood, captive, desolated
Rome was consoled by the reborn hope.
Before being yours, we were her children.
I am thinking of your power; but think of your oaths.

BRUTUS:

Yes, let Caesar be great; but let Rome be free.
Gods! Mistress of the Indus, but slave at the shore of
    the Tiber:
What matter that her name commands the universe:
And that she's called queen, although she is in fetters!
What matter to my country, to the Romans that you
    brave,
To learn that Caesar has new slaves?
The Persians are not our fiercest enemies;
There is one greater. I have no other opinion.

CAESAR:

And, you Brutus, also.

ANTHONY: (to Caesar)

You know their audacity.
See if these ingrate hearts are worthy of your mercy.

CAESAR:

So then, in your boldness, you wish
To tempt my patience and to give up my bounties?
You who belong to me by the right of the sword,
Rampant under Marius, slaves of Pompey,
You who breathe only because my wrath,
Restrained too long, stops over you.
Ungrateful republicans who, emboldened by my clem-
    ency,
You, who before Sulla kept silent,
You who my beneficence alone invites to outrage me
Without fear that Caesar will stoop to avenge himself.
So that's what gives you a soul bold enough
To dare to speak to me of Rome and country;
To affect here this illustrious hauteur
And these grand sentiments before your conqueror.
It lacked them on the plains of Pharsalia
Fortune between us became very unequal.

If you don't know how to conquer learn to serve.

BRUTUS:

Caesar, none of us knows anything accept to die.
None of us I disavow, and none, in Thessaly,
Lowered his courage to request his life.
You left us life, but to debase us
And we detest it if you must be obeyed.
Caesar, let none of us escape your wrath.
Start here with me; if you wish to reign, strike.

CAESAR:

Listen and you leave.

(the Senators leave)

Brutus dares to offend me!
But do you know with what darts you've just pierced
    me?
Go, Caesar is very far from wishing to kill you.
Leave there, the indiscreet fury of the Senate.
Remain, it's you alone who can disarm me.
Stay, it's you alone Caesar wants to love.

BRUTUS:

All my blood is yours if you keep your promise.
If you are only a tyrant, I abhor your tenderness.
And I can no longer remain with Anthony and you
Since he's no longer Roman and he asks for a king.

(Exit Brutus.)

ANTHONY:

Well! Did I deceive you? Do you think that nature
Can mollify a soul so proud and hard?
Leave, leave forever in its obscurity
This wretched secret which weighs on your kindness.
As for Rome, if he wishes, let him deplore the fall.
But let him remain unaware of what blood he is perse-
    cuting.
He doesn't deserve to owe you life,
Ingrate to all your bounties, ingrate to your love.
Renounce him for your son.

CAESAR:

I cannot; I love him.

ANTHONY:

Ah! Then cease to love the dazzle of the diadem.
Descend then from the rung to which I've seen you
climb.
Kindness sits ill with your authority;
It destroys the work of your burgeoning grandeur.
What! Rome is under your sway, and Cassius outrages
you!
What! Cimber, what! Cinna, and these obscure
Senators,
To affect these hauteurs to the eyes of the king of the
world!
They brave your power and these vanquished still
breath!

CAESAR:

They were born my equals, my arms conquered them,
And, very much above them, I can pardon them
For boiling under the yoke I wish to place on them

ANTHONY:

Marius would have been less thrifty of their blood.
Sulla would have punished them.

CAESAR:

Sulla was a barbarian;
He only knew how to oppress. Murder and fury
Were his politics as much as his grandeur.
He governed Rome in the midst of tortures.
He was their terror, I will be their delight.
I know what the people are: they change in a day.
They lavish their hate and their love.
If my grandeur exasperates, my clemency attracts.
A politic pardon to one who cannot injure me, and
Is in my fetters, wearing them with an air of liberty,
Has brought towards me his weak will.
I must cover with flowers the abyss into which I am
    dragging them,
Once more flatter the tiger at the moment he's being
    enchained.
Pleasing him in crushing him, charming him
And punishing my rivals by making myself loved.

ANTHONY:

It's necessary to be feared; that's how you reign.

CAESAR:

Go, it's only in battles that I want to be feared.

ANTHONY:

The people will abuse your easiness.

CAESAR:

Up to now the people have sanctified my bounty.
See this temple Rome has raised to clemency.

ANTHONY:

Beware they don't raise another to vengeance.
Beware of ulcerated hearts nourished in despair.
Idolaters of Rome and cruel by duty,
Alarmed Cassius foresees that this very day
My hand must place the diadem on your head.
Already, even before your eyes they dare to murmur.
Of more impetuous ones you must assure yourself.
To prevent their blows, at least deign to contradict
    yourself.

CAESAR:

I would have punished them if I were able to fear
    them.
Don't advise me to make myself hated.
I know how to fight, conquer, and don't know how to

punish.

Let's go, and listening to neither suspicion nor vengeance,

Let's reign over the universe without violence.

CURTAIN

ACT II

ANTHONY:

This proud refusal, this animosity,
Reveal less virtue than ferocity.
The kindness of Caesar, and especially his power
Deserve better consideration and more complaisance.
You could agree to speak to him less.
You don't know who you dare hate,
And you would be shivering from it if you knew.

BRUTUS:

Ah! I'm shivering already; but it's from hearing you.
Enemy of Romans that you've betrayed,
Can you imagine to deceive or corrupt Brutus?
Go, crawl without me under the hand that braves you.
I know all your plans, you are burning to be a slave,
You are a Roman and you want a monarch!

ANTHONY:

I am a friend, Brutus, and I bear a humane heart:
I am not seeking after any rare virtue.
You want to be a hero, go, you are only a barbarian.
And your savage pride, which nothing can soften
Embraces virtue in a way to make it hated.

(Exit Anthony.)

BRUTUS:

What baseness, o heaven, and what ignominy!
Now there are the supports of my sorrowing country!
Behold your successors, Horace, Decimus,
And you avenger of the laws, you, my blood, you,
   Brutus!
Just gods, what remains of Roman Grandeur!
Trembling, everyone kisses the hand that enchains us.
Caesar has raped us even of our virtues;
And here I am seeking Rome and no longer find it.
I've seen you perish, you immortals of courage;
Heroes, whose images I see weeping,
Family of Pompey, and you, divine Cato,
You, last of the heroes, of Scipio's blood,
You revive in me these vivid sparks
Of virtues with which your immortal souls shone.
You live in Brutus, you put in my breast

All the honor that a tyrant ravishes from the name of
Roman.
Great Pompey, what do I see at the foot of your
shadow?
What letter addressed to me is presented to my sight?
Let's read: "You are sleeping, Brutus, and Rome is in
fetters."
Rome, my eyes on you will always be open.
Don't reproach me for the chains I abhor.
But what other letter is offering itself to my eyes once
more?
"No, you are not Brutus." Ah! Cruel reproach!
Caesar! Tremble tyrant! Now there's your mortal
blow.
"No, you are not Brutus!" I am, I want to be him.
Romans I will perish or you will be without a master.
I see that Rome still has virtuous hearts.
They demand an avenger, their eyes are on me.
They excite this soul, and this too tardy hand.
They demand blood. Rome will be satisfied.

**(Enter Cassius, Cinna, Casca, Decimus, and their
followers.)**

CASSIUS:

I am embracing you, Brutus, for the last time.
Friend, I must fall under the debris of the laws.

From Caesar, henceforth, I expect no mercy.
He knows my feelings, he knows our audacity.
Our incorruptible soul astonishes his plans.
In us, he is going to ruin the last of the Romans.
It's over, my friends, there's no more country,
No more honor, no more laws: Rome's been annihi-
    lated.
Of the universe over which he's triumphing today,
Our imprudent ancestors conquered it only for him.
These spoils of kings, this scepter of the earth,
Six hundred years of virtue, of toil, and of war.
Caesar enjoys it all and devours the fruit.
All six centuries of glory labored to produce.
Ah! Brutus! Were you born to serve under a master?
Liberty is no more.

BRUTUS:

It's ready to be reborn.

CASSIUS:

What are you saying? But what uproar assaults my
    spirit?

BRUTUS:

Leave there, the vile populace and its unworthy
   screaming.

CASSIUS:

Liberty, you say? But what? The noise is increasing.

(Enter Cimber.)

CASSIUS:

Ah! Cimber, is it you? Speak, what's this disturbance?

DECIMUS:

Are they plotting a new a outrage against Rome?
What are they doing? What have you seen?

CIMBER:

The disgrace of the State.
Caesar was at the temple and this proud idol
Seems to be the god who thunders from the Capitol.

It's there that he announced his superb plan
To join Persia to the Roman empire.
They gave him the name Lightning of War,
Avenger of Romans, Conqueror of the Earth.
But amongst so much outburst, his imprudent pride
Wanted another title, and wasn't satisfied.
At last amongst those shouts and songs of glee
From people who surrounded him, Anthony pushed
    through the crowd.
He enters: o shame! O crime unworthy of a Roman!
He enters, crown and scepter in hand.
They shut up, they shivered:
He, on the head of Caesar places the crown,
And suddenly, before him, hurls himself on his knees
"Caesar, he says, reign over the earth and over us."
At these words, some Romans' faces paled.
The vaults of heaven resounded with their dolorous
    shouts.
I saw some citizens fleeing with horror.
Others blushed with shame and wept with sorrow.
Caesar, who still read on their face
The bursting evidence of indignation
Feigning long practiced sentiments
Tossed away scepter and crown and trampled them
    under his feet.
Then all think themselves free, when all are in jeop-
    ardy,
A madman intoxicated with indiscreet joy.
Anthony was alarmed; Caesar feigned and blushed;
Then he concealed his trouble, and the more they

applauded it,
Moderation served to veil his crime.
He affected to regret a magnanimous refusal.
But despite his efforts, he shivered underneath
As they applauded in him virtues that he doesn't have.
Still, no longer being able to restrain his wrath,
He left the Capitol with a severe look.
He intends that in an hour the Senate should reassemble.
Brutus, in an hour Caesar is changing the State.
With the Senate half corrupted,
Having bought Rome, they're selling it to Caesar.
More cowardly than the people who in its misfortune
The name of king at least has always somewhat horrified.
Caesar, already too much king, still wants the crown.
The people are refusing it, the Senate will give it to him
In the end, heroes who are listening to me—what must be done?

CASSIUS:

Die, and end our lives of oppressive calculations.
I've dragged chains throughout my unworthy life
So long as a little hope flattered my country.
Behold its last day, and, Cassius, at least
Doesn't want to breath when the State is no more.
Weep whoever wants Rome, and remain faithful to

her.
I can no longer avenge her, but I can expire with her.
I am going where our gods are.

(looking at their statues)

Pompey and Scipio,
It's time to follow you and to imitate Cato.

BRUTUS:

No, let's not imitate anybody,
And let's serve all as an example
The universe is contemplating us, brave friends.
It's up to us to answer to the admiration
That expiring Rome preserves for our name.
If Cato had listened to me, he would have lost his life
More justly in his fury over expiring Caesar.
But he turned on himself his innocent hands.
His death was useless to the good of mankind.
Doing everything for glory, he did nothing for Rome,
And it's the only error this great man fell into.

CASSIUS:

What do you expect someone to do in such despair?

BRUTUS:

This is what they wrote me, that's our duty.

CASSIUS:

They wrote me, too; I received this reproach.

BRUTUS:

It's too much to deserve it.

CIMBER:

The fatal hour approaches.
In an hour the tyrant will destroy the name "Roman."

BRUTUS:

In an hour it's necessary to pierce his breast.

CASSIUS:

Ah! I recognize in this your noble audacity.

DECIMUS:

Enemy of tyrants, and worthy of your race
Now those are the feelings I had in my heart.

CASSIUS:

You deliver them to me myself, and I owe you the
    honor of it.
That's what my hate and my rage was expecting
Of the male strength that forms your character.
It's Rome that inspires in you these grand designs.
Your name alone is the decree of death to tyrants.
My dear Brutus let's wash the opprobrium from the
    earth
Let's avenge this Capitol, in want of thunder.
You, Cimber, you Cinna, you dauntless Romans,
Do you have any other soul and any other will?

CIMBER:

We think like you, we scorn life;
We detest Caesar, we love our country.
We all will avenge it: Brutus and Cassius
Are reviving the virtues of whatever is Roman.

DECIMUS:

Born judges of the State, born avengers of crime,
Too long suffering the hand that oppresses us,
And if on a tyrant we suspend our blows
For us each moment that he breathes is a crime for us.

CIMBER:

Shall we admit someone else into this supreme honor?

BRUTUS:

We ourselves suffice to avenge the country.
Dolabella, Lepidus, Emilius, Bibulus,
Either tremble under Caesar or indeed have sold out to
    him.
Cicero who once punished the insolence of a traitor
Serves liberty only with his eloquence;
Bold in the Senate, weak in danger,
Made to harangue Rome and not to avenge her.
Let's leave to the orator who charms his country
The duty of praising us after we have served it.
No, it's only with you I wish to share
This immortal honor and this pressing danger.
The Senate must surrender to the tyrant in an hour.
There, I will punish him; there, I intend to surprise
    him.

There, I intend this dagger thrust into his breast
To avenge Cato, Pompey, and the Roman people.
It's hazarding much. His passionate adherents
Occupy the limits of the Capitol.
This indolent people, flighty and easy to mollify,
Doesn't yet know if it must love him or hate him.
Our death, my friends seems inevitable.
But how noble and desirable is such a death.
How fine it is to perish in plans so great.
To see his blood shed in the blood of tyrants!
With what pleasure then we'll see his last hour!
Let's die, brave friends, so long as Caesar dies.
And so that Liberty, oppressed by his misdeeds,
Will be reborn from its ashes and revive forever.

CASSIUS:

Let's not hesitate any further, let's run to the Capitol.
It's there that he oppresses us and it's there he must be
    sacrificed.
Let's not fear the people at all, they seem still unde-
    cided,
But if the idol falls, they are going to detest it.

BRUTUS:

Then swear with me, swear on this sword,
By the blood of Cato and Pompey,

By the sacred manes of all true Romans
That in the fields of Africa ended their destinies,
Swear by all the gods, avengers of the country,
That Caesar will end his life beneath your blows.

CASSIUS:

My friends, do more. Let's swear to exterminate
Whoever thus pretends to govern Rome,
Be it our own sons, our brothers or our fathers.
Brutus, if they are tyrants, they are our adversaries.
A true republican has for father and sons
Only virtue, the gods, the laws, and his country.

BRUTUS:

Yes, I am uniting my blood with yours forever.
From this moment all are adopting each other;
The good of the state has made us relatives.
Let's seal our union with the blood of tyrants.

(advancing towards the statue of Pompey)

We are swearing by you, hero, whose image
Excites our courage to this urgent duty.
Pompey, at your sacred knees we promise
To do everything for Rome and nothing for ourselves.
To be united in the State which reassembles in us,

To live, to fight, to die together.
Let's go, let's prepare ourselves, it's too much to stop
  ourselves.

(All the conspirators are leaving. Caesar enters and sees Brutus.)

CAESAR:

Stay put, it's here you must listen to me.
Where are you going, wretch?

BRUTUS:

Far from tyranny.

CAESAR:

Lictors, keep him here.

BRUTUS:

Be done with it and take my life.

CAESAR:

Brutus, if my anger extended to your life;
I wouldn't talk, I'd end its course.
You are too meritorious. Your proud ingratitude
Offends me with a sullen deliberation.
Again I find you with those Romans
Whom I most suspect of perfidious plans.
With those who just dared to displease me,
Having blamed my conduct, having braved my wrath.

BRUTUS:

Caesar, they are speaking like Romans, and their opin-
    ions
Would be followed if the gods inspired you.

CAESAR:

I suffer your audacity, and consent to listen to you.
With you I am pleased to descend from my rank,
With what do you reproach me?

BRUTUS:

The ravaged world,
The blood of nations, the pillage of your country;

Your power, your virtues which form your injustices
Which by your outrages are accomplices in you.
Your funereal generosity that makes your fetters loved
And which are only a bait with which to deceive the
    universe.

CAESAR:

Ah! That's what Pompey should have been reproached
    for.
With his feigned virtue yours was deceived.
That proud citizen, to Rome most fatal,
Never wanted Caesar to be his equal.
Do you think if he had conquered me, his haughty
    soul
Would have let Roman liberty breathe?
He would have overwhelmed you under his despotic
    yoke.
What would Brutus have done then?

BRUTUS:

Brutus would have sacrificed him.

CAESAR:

Now that's what your great heart is destining for me in

the end.
Don't defend yourself over it. You are living for my
   ruin, Brutus!

BRUTUS:

If you believe that, forestall my fury.
Who can restrain you?

CAESAR: (presenting him with Servilia's letter)

Nature, and my heart.
Read, ingrate, read; learn the blood that you are
   opposing me with.
See who you can hate and go ahead if you dare.

BRUTUS:

Where am I? What have I read? Are my eyes deceiving
   me?

CAESAR:

Well, Brutus, my son?

BRUTUS:

Him, my father! Great gods!

CAESAR:

Yes, that I am, ingrate! What wild silence!
What do I say? What sobs are escaping your mouth?
My son— What! I hold you mute between my arms!
Nature astonishes you, and doesn't soften you!

BRUTUS:

O terrifying fate that makes me desperate.
O oaths! O country! O always cherished Rome!
Caesar! Ah! Wretchedness! I have lived too long.

CAESAR:

Speak. What! Your heart is fighting with remorse.
Don't conceal anything from me. You are keeping
   silent.
Don't fear to be my son;
That sacred name offends you.
You fear being cherished by me, of sharing my rank.
It's a misfortune for you to be born of my blood.
Ah! This scepter over the world, and this supreme

power
This Caesar that you hate, want them for yourself.
I want to share, with Octavius and you
The reward of a hundred battles, and the title of king.

BRUTUS:

Ah, gods!

CAESAR:

You want to speak and you are having trouble control-
ling yourself.
Are these distractions from tenderness or hatred?
Now, what is this secret that seems to overwhelm you?

BRUTUS:

Caesar—

CAESAR:

Well, my son?

BRUTUS:

I cannot tell it.

CAESAR:

You don't dare to call me by the tender name of father?

BRUTUS:

If you are, I make one sole prayer to you.

CAESAR:

Speak: by granting it to you, I will hope to win everything.

BRUTUS:

Make me die on the spot or cease to reign.

CAESAR:

Ah! Barbarous enemy, tiger that I am caressing!
Ah! Unnatural heart which hardens my tenderness!

Go, you are no longer my son. Go, cruel citizen.
My despairing heart takes example from yours.
This heart which you terribly injured
Will indeed know how to vanquish nature in the end.
Go, Caesar wasn't made to pray to you in vain.
I will learn from Brutus how to stop being humane.
I won't know you any more. Free in my power
I will no longer listen to unjust clemency.
Calmly, I'm going to abandon myself to my wrath.
My too indulgent heart is weary of pardoning.
I will imitate Sulla, but in his worst violence.
Ingrates, you will tremble at the rumor of my
    vengeance.
Go, cruel one, go find your unworthy friends.
All who have dared to displease me, they will all be
    punished.
They know what I can do; they will see what I dare.
I will become barbarous, and you alone are the cause.

BRUTUS:

Ah! Let's not leave him in such cruel thoughts,
If we can, let's save Caesar and Rome!

(Brutus rushes after Caesar.)

CURTAIN

ACT III

CASSIUS:

At last the hour approaches in which Rome will be
    reborn.
The mistress of the world is today without a master.
The honor in it is yours, Cimber, Casca, Probus,
Decimus. Just one more hour and the tyrant is no
    more.
What Cato, and Pompey, and Asia were unable to
    do—
We alone will execute him, we will avenge the country,
And on this day I want it to be said to the universe:
"Mortals, respect Rome, she's no longer in chains."

CIMBER:

You see all our friends are ready to follow you.
To strike, to die, to live if we must live,
To serve the Senate in either fate
By giving death to Caesar or receiving it from him.

DECIMUS:

But why hasn't Brutus yet appeared?
He, this fierce enemy of the tyrant he abhors,
He who received our oaths, who brought us all
    together,
He who must lay the first blow on Caesar,
The son-in-law of Cato is really slow to appear.
Could he have been arrested? Perhaps Caesar knows.
But here he is. Great gods! How defeated he seems!

(Enter Brutus.)

CASSIUS:

Brutus, what ill fortune overwhelms your virtue?

Does the tyrant know? Is Rome betrayed?

BRUTUS:

No.
Caesar doesn't know that we're going to cut short his
    life.
He trusts in you.

DECIMUS:

Then what can be disturbing you like this?

BRUTUS:

A misfortune, a secret, which will make you tremble.

CASSIUS:

Death is readying itself for us or the tyrant.
We may all perish, but tremble, us!

BRUTUS:

Stop.
I am going to shock you with this horrifying secret.
I owe his death to Rome, to you, to your descendants,
To the happiness of mortals, I've chosen the time,
The place, the arm, the moment in which Rome wants
   him to die
The honor of the first blow is confided to my hands.
Everything is ready: know that Brutus is his son.

CIMBER:

You, his son!

CASSIUS:

Of Caesar!

DECIMUS:

O Rome!

BRUTUS:

Servilia
Was joined to Caesar in a secret marriage.
I am the unfortunate fruit of that marriage.

CIMBER:

Brutus, son of a tyrant!

CASSIUS:

No, you weren't born of him.

Your heart is too Roman.

BRUTUS:

My shame is real.
You, friends, who see the destiny that overwhelms
    me,
Will be by my oaths the masters of my fate.
Is there one of you with a spirit strong enough,
Stoic enough, enough above the vulgar,
To dare to decide what Brutus must do?
I deliver myself to you. What! You are lowering your
    eyes!
You, Cassius, too, you are silent like them!
None can support to the shore of this abyss!
None encourages me, or snatches me from the crime.
You shiver, Cassius! And prompt to astonish you—

CASSIUS:

I am shivering with the advice I must give you.

BRUTUS:

Speak.

CASSIUS:

If you were only a common citizen,
I would say to you: Go, serve, be tyrant under your
    father;
Destroy the state you ought to support.
Henceforth Rome will have two traitors to punish.
But I am speaking to Brutus, to this powerful genius,
To this hero armed against tyranny,
Whose inflexible heart, determined on the best,
Will purify the blood Caesar has given you.
Listen, you know with what fury
Cataline once threatened his country?

BRUTUS:

Yes.

CASSIUS:

If, the very day that this great criminal
Intended to deliver a mortal blow to liberty,
If, after The Senate condemned this traitor,
Cataline had wanted to recognize you for his son,
Forced to choose between that monster and us,
Speak, what would you have decided?

BRUTUS:

Can you ask?
Do you think that for an instant my disappointed
  virtue
Would have hesitated for a minute between man and
  country?

CASSIUS:

Brutus, your duty is dictated by that single word.
It's the decree of the Senate, Rome is secure.
But, speak, are you feeling this unease and this secret
  murmur
That a vulgar prejudice imputes to nature?
Has a single word from Caesar extinguished in you
Your love of country, your duty, your faith?
By telling this secret, whether true or false
By admitting you as son, is he any less guilty?
Are you less Brutus? Are you less Roman?
Do you owe us your life, your heart and your hand any
  less?
You, his son! In the end is Rome no longer your
  mother?
In that case is each of the conspirators no longer your
  brother?
Born in our sacred walls, nourished by Scipio,
Raised by Pompey, adopted by Cato,
Friend of Cassius, what more do you want?

These titles are sacred: all others outrage them.
What's it matter that a tyrant, enslaved by love,
Seduced Servilia, and you were given life?
Leave there, the sins and marriage of your mother;
Cato formed your morals; Cato alone is your father.
You owe him your virtue; your soul is completely his.
Break the unworthy fetter you are being offered today.
Let your firmness answer to our common oaths.
And you have no relatives except the avengers of the
    world.

BRUTUS:

And you, brave friends, speak, what are you thinking?

CIMBER:

Judge us by him, judge him by us.
If we were capable of another sentiment
Rome would not need more guilty children.
But to others than yourself, why give an account?
It's your heart, it's Brutus you must consult.

BRUTUS:

Well, to your observation my soul is revealed.
Read in it the horrors by which it is overwhelmed.

I am concealing nothing from you, this heart is shaken,
Tears have poured from my stoic eyes.
After the frightful oath you saw me take,
Ready to serve the State, but to kill my father:
Weeping to be his son, shamed by his bounties,
Admiring his virtues, condemning his crimes,
Seeing my father in him, a guilty but great man,
Swept away by Caesar, held fast by Rome.
My soul is torn apart by horror and pity
Wishing the death that you are preparing for him.
I will tell you even more; know that I esteem him
His great heart is seducing me even to the breast of
    crime,
And if someone could reign over Romans,
He is the only tyrant that they ought to spare.
Don't be alarmed: that's the name I detest,
Merely the name of tyrant decides the rest.
The Senate, Rome and you, have my word.
The well being of the whole world speaks to me against
    a king.
With horror I am embracing a cruel virtue.
I am shivering with it before your eyes, but I am faithful
    to you.
Caesar is going to speak to me: may I not today
Soften him, change him, save the State and him?
The immortals will it, explaining by my mouth,
Loaning to my tongue a power that will touch him!
But if I obtain nothing from his ambition,
Raise your arm, strike, I will turn my eyes away.
I will not betray my country for my father.

Approve it or not, my strict firmness endures.
Let the astonished universe approve or not this great
    action,
Be it an object of horror or admiration.
My spirit little jealous of surviving in memory
Considers neither reproach nor glory.
Always independent and ever the citizen,
My duty suffices me, all the rest is nothing.
Go, don't think any further except of leaving slavery.

CASSIUS:

Of the security of the state your word is your pledge.
We are all counting on you, as if we heard
Cato, Rome itself and our gods hereabouts.

(The conspirators leave.)

BRUTUS:

Now's the moment Caesar's going to listen to me.
Here's the Capitol where death is going to await him.
Spare me, great gods, the horror of hating him!
Gods, stop these arms raised to punish him!
Return, if it's possible, his great and most dear heart
    to Rome,
And make him be just, so that he can be my father!

Here he is! I remain motionless, distracted.
O manes of Cato, sustain my virtue!

(Enter Caesar.)

CAESAR:

Well! What do you want? Speak. Do you have the heart
    of a man?
Are you the son of Caesar?

BRUTUS:

Yes, if you are the son of Rome.

CAESAR:

Wild republican, where are you going to lead your-
    self?
Do you want to see me only to better insult me?
What! While my favors are showered over you,
As the world's submissive homage awaits you,
Empire, my bounties, nothing softens your heart?
With what eye then do you view the scepter?

BRUTUS:

With horror.

CAESAR:

I pity your prejudices, I even excuse them.
But can you hate me?

BRUTUS:

No, Caesar, and I love you.
My heart was biased towards you by your exploits
Before your blood made me recognize you.
I am pitied by the gods to see such a great man
Made at once the glory and the scourge of Rome.
I detest Caesar with the name of king,
But Citizen Caesar would be a god for me.
I would sacrifice my fortune for him and my life.

CAESAR:

What is there about me you can hate?

BRUTUS:

Tyranny.
Deign to listen to the prayers, the tears, the opinions,
Of all true Romans, of the Senate, of your son.
Do you indeed wish to live the first on earth,
To enjoy by a right more holy than that of war,
To be yet more than king, yet even more than Caesar?

CAESAR:

Well?

BRUTUS:

You will see the earth enchained to your chariot.
Break our fetters, be Roman, renounce the diadem.

CAESAR:

Ah! What are you proposing?

BRUTUS:

What even Sulla did.
Sulla bathed a long while in our blood.

He rendered Rome free, and all was forgotten.
That illustrious murderer, surrounded by victims,
By descending from the throne erased all his crimes.
You do not have his furors, dare to have his virtues.
Your heart knows how to pardon; Caesar, do yet more.
Henceforth what's the use of the mercies you dispense?
It's Rome, the State, you must pardon.
Then, more than to your rank our hearts will be submis-
    sive to you;
Then you will know how to reign, then I am your son.
What! Am I speaking to you in vain?

CAESAR:

Rome demands a master.
Perhaps one day you will learn it at your expense.
You see our citizens more powerful than kings.
Our morals are changing, Brutus, we must change our
    laws.
Liberty is no longer anything but the right to injure.
Rome which destroyed everything,
Seems finally to be destroying itself.
This terrifying colossus by which the world is tram-
    pled,
By shaking the universe is itself shaken.
It's leaning towards its fall, and against the storm
It demands my arm to keep its head.
In the end, since Sulla, our ancient virtues,
The laws, Rome, the state, are superfluous names.

In our corrupted times, filled with civil wars,
You are speaking as if in the times of Decimus,
  Emilius.
Cato has seduced you too much, my dear son: I foresee
That your sad virtue will ruin the state and you.
If you can, let your deceived reason give in
To the conqueror of Cato, to the conqueror of Pompey,
To your father who loves you and who pities your
  mistake.
Be my son indeed, Brutus, give me your heart;
Adopt other feelings, my bounty conjures you.
Don't force your soul to vanquish nature.
You don't answer me at all. You turn your eyes away?

BRUTUS:

I don't know you any more. Thunder on me, great
  gods!
Caesar—

CAESAR:

What! You're moved? Your soul is mollified?
Ah! My son—

BRUTUS:

Do you really know this goes to your life!
Do you know for sure that the Senate has no true
  Roman
Who aspires in secret to pierce your breast?
That the safety of Rome, and yours touch?
Your alarmed genius is speaking to you through my
  mouth.
It pushes me, it urges me, it tosses me at your feet.

(he throws himself at his knees)

Caesar, in the name of the gods, in your forgetful
  heart,
In the name of your virtues, of Rome, and of yourself,
Speaking in the name of a son who shivers and who
  loves you,
Don't rebuff me!

CAESAR:

Wretch, leave me alone.
What do you want from me?

BRUTUS:

Believe me, don't be insensitive.

CAESAR:

The universe can change; my soul is inflexible.

BRUTUS:

Then that's your reply?

CAESAR:

Yes, it's all decided.
Rome must obey when Caesar wills it.

BRUTUS: (in a confounded way)

Goodbye, Caesar.

CAESAR:

Hey, what! Where are these tears coming from?
Stay awhile, my son! What! You are shedding tears!
What! Brutus can weep! Is it over having a king?
Are you weeping for Romans?

BRUTUS:

I am only weeping for you.
Goodbye, I tell you.

(Exit Brutus.)

CAESAR:

O Rome! O heroic fortitude!
Now why can't I love my republic to this degree?

(Enter Dolabella with Romans.)

DOLABELLA:

By your order the Senate has arrived at the temple.
They are only waiting for you; the throne is erected.
All those who have sold their lives and their votes for
    you
Are going to squander incense at the feet of your
    statues.
I am bringing before you the Roman crowd.
The Senate is going to decide their uncertain minds.
But if Caesar will believe a citizen who loves him
Our terrible omens, our diviners, even our gods,

Caesar will put off this great event.

CAESAR:

What! If it's necessary to reign, to defer it for a
    moment!
Who could stop me, me?

DOLABELLA:

All nature
Conspires to warn you by a sinister augury.
Heaven, which makes kings, worries over your death.

CAESAR:

Go, Caesar is only a man and I don't think
That heaven is uneasy to such a degree about my fate
That it animates for me mute nature
And the elements appear confused
For a mortal to breath one more day.
In high heaven the gods have counted our years.
Let's follow without recoil our lofty destiny.
Caesar has nothing to fear.

DOLABELLA:

He has enemies
Who have hardly submitted to a new yoke.
Who knows to what degree they are conspiring their
  vengeance?

CAESAR:

They wouldn't dare.

DOLABELLA:

Your heart is too full of confidence.

CAESAR:

Too many precautions against my fatal day
Will make me derided, and ill protect me.

DOLABELLA:

Caesar must live for the well-being of Rome.
At least permit me to follow you into the Senate.

CAESAR:

No, why change the order agreed to between us?
Don't come any further friend, the moment directs:
He who changes his plans reveals his weakness.

DOLABELLA:

I am leaving you regretfully, I'm worried, I admit it.
This new feeling in my heart is very strong.

CAESAR:

Go, I prefer to die than to fear death.
Let's get going.

(Caesar goes into the Senate.)

DOLABELLA: (to the Romans)

Dear citizens, what hero, what courage,
On earth is more deserving of your homage?
People who admire him, join your prayers with mine.
Confirm the honors prepared for him,
Live to serve him, die to defend him.
What clamors, o heaven, what shouts are being heard!

THE CONSPIRATORS: (behind the scenes)

Die, expire, tyrant! Courage, Cassius!

DOLABELLA:

Ah! Let's rush to save him.

(Enter Cassius, dagger in hand.)

CASSIUS:

It's over; he is no more.

DOLABELLA:

People, second me: let's strike, let's skewer this traitor.

CASSIUS:

People, imitate me, you no longer have a master.
Nation of heroes, conquerors of the universe,
Long live liberty! My hand broke your chains.

DOLABELLA:

Romans, will you betray the blood of this great man?

CASSIUS:

I killed my friend for the good of Rome!
He enslaved you all, his blood is shed,
Is there one of you with so little virtue,
With such a cringing spirit, with such a feeble courage,
That he can regret Caesar and slavery?
Who is this vile Roman who wished to have a king?
If there is one, let him speak and let him complain of
    me.
But you who are applauding me, you all love glory.

ROMANS:

Caesar was a tyrant; let his memory perish.

CASSIUS:

Masters of the whole world, happy children of Rome,
Preserve these noble sentiments forever.
I know that Anthony is going to appear before you.
Friends, remember that Caesar was his master,
That he served under him from his earliest youth

In a school of crime and the art of tyranny.
He's coming to justify his crime and his empire.
He despises you enough to think of seducing you.
No question, he can make his voice heard here.
Such is the law of Rome and I obey its laws.
The people are henceforth the supreme tongue,
The judge of Caesar, of Anthony, and of myself.
You are resuming your inheritance, unworthily lost.
Caesar ravished them from you, I've returned them to
    you.
I want to affirm them. I am going back into the Capitol
Brutus is in the Senate. He's awaiting me, and I'm
    rushing to him.
I am going with Brutus, in these desolate walls,
To recall justice and our exiled gods.
To suffocate evil intestine furors,
And to repair the ruins of liberty.
You, Romans, merely consent to be happy.
Don't betray yourself, that's all I desire.
Suspect Anthony completely, and especially trickery.

ROMANS:

If he dares to accuse you, he himself will perish.

CASSIUS:

Remember, Romans, these sacred oaths.

ROMANS:

To the avengers of the State our hearts are sealed.

(Exit Cassius back into the Senate.)

ROMAN:

But Anthony is appearing.

ANOTHER ROMAN:

What will he dare to say to us?

A ROMAN:

His eyes are shedding tears; he's upset, he's sighing.

ANOTHER:

He loved Caesar too much.

ANTHONY: (entering and mounting the tribune to harangue them)

Yes, Romans, I loved him.
Yes, with my life I would have prolonged his destiny.
Alas! You've all thought as I felt myself;
And when removing the diadem from his head,
This hero sacrificed himself to your laws today.
Which of you, indeed, would not have expired for
   him?
Alas! I am not coming to celebrate his memory;
The whole world's voice speaks enough of his glory.
But of my despair, at least have some pity,
And at least forgive the tears of friendship.

A ROMAN:

He made them pour out when Rome had a master.
Caesar was a hero, but Caesar was a traitor.

ANOTHER ROMAN:

After he became a tyrant he no longer had any virtues.

A THIRD:

Yes, we all approve of Cassius and Brutus.

ANTHONY:

Against these murderers I have nothing to say to you.
It was to serve the state that their great heart aspired.
They pierced the side of your great dictator.
Filled with his benefits, they are stained by his blood.
To force Romans to this despicable act,
No question, Caesar must have been very guilty.
I believe it. But still, did Caesar ever
Weigh you down with the power of the fasces?
Did he keep for himself the fruit of his conquests?
With the spoils of the world he crowned your heads.
All the gold of the nations which fell under his blows,
All the prizes of his blood were produced for you.
From his triumphal chariot he saw your alarms;
Caesar descended from it to dry your tears.
You triumph peacefully over the world he subdued,
Powerful through his courage, happy through his
    blessings,
He paid for services, he pardoned outrage.
Great gods, you know him! you in whose image he
    was made;
Gods, you who allowed him to govern the world,
You know if his heart loved to pardon!

ROMANS:

It's true that Caesar did love his clemency.

ANTHONY:

Alas! If his great soul had known vengeance,
He would be living and his life would have fulfilled
　　our desires.
On all his murderers he showered his benefits.
Twice he saved Cassius' life.
Brutus—where am I? O heaven, o crime, o barbarity!
Dear friends, I am succumbing, and my speechless
　　senses—
Brutus, his assassin! That monster was his son!

ROMANS:

Ah, gods!

ANTHONY:

I see your generous courage shiver;
Friends, I see the tears that moisten your faces.
Yes, Brutus is his son; but you who are listening to
　　me,
You were his children in his adopted heart.
Alas! If you knew his last will!

ROMANS:

What is it? Speak.

ANTHONY:

Rome is his heir.
His treasures are your wealth; you are going to enjoy
     it all.
Even from the tomb, Caesar wants to serve you.
It's you alone that he loved; it's for you, that in Asia,
He was going to lavish his fortune and his life.
"O Romans," he said, "kingly people that I serve,
Command Caesar, as Caesar the universe."
Brutus or Cassius would have done more?

ROMANS:

Ah! We detest them. This suspicion outrages us.

A ROMAN:

Caesar was indeed the father of the state.

ANTHONY:

Your father is no more. A cowardly assassination
Just cut short the life of this great man,
The honor of nature and the glory of Rome.
Romans, will you deprive yourselves of the honors of
   the funeral pyre
Of this father, this friend, who was so dear to you?
They are bringing him before your eyes.

(The back of the stage opens; Lictors carry in the body of Caesar covered with a bloody sheet; Anthony comes down from the podium and casts himself on his knees by the body.)

ROMANS:

O funereal spectacle!

ANTHONY:

See what remains to you of the greatest of Romans.
Behold this vengeful god, idolized by you,
That even his assassins adored on their knees,
Who, ever your support in peace and in war,
An hour before made the earth tremble,
Who ought to have enchained Babylon to his chariot:

Friends, in this condition do you know Caesar?
See then, Romans, touch these wounds,
This blood shed before your eyes by perjured hands,
There, Cimber struck him: there on the great Caesar
Cassius and Decimus thrust in their daggers.
There, bewildered Brutus, Brutus, soul distracted,
Soiled his unnatural hand in these flanks.
Caesar, looking at him with a calm and soft eye,
Pardoned him again, falling under his blows.
He called him his son; and this dear and tender name
Is the only one that in dying Caesar uttered.
"O my son!" he said.

A ROMAN:

O monster that the gods
Should have exterminated before this frightful blow.

OTHER ROMANS: (looking at the body which they
  are near)

Gods! His blood is still pouring out.

ANTHONY:

He's demanding vengeance.
He's expecting it from your hands and your valor.

Can you hear his voice? Wake up, Romans.
March, follow me against his assassins.
Those are the honors you must render Caesar.
With brands from the funeral pyre
That is going to turn him into ashes,
Let's fire the palaces of these proud conspirators.
Let's shove our desperate arms through their breasts.
Come, worthy friends, come avengers of crimes,
To the god of the country sacrifice these victims.

ROMANS:

Yes, we will punish them, yes, we will follow on your
    heels.
We swear by his blood to avenge his death.
Let's hurry.

ANTHONY: (to Dolabella)

Let's not let their fury be wasted.
Let's rush this inconstant and easy people;
Drag them to war and without undue caution
Let's succeed Caesar by rushing to avenge him.

CURTAIN

ABOUT THE AUTHOR

Frank J. Morlock has written and translated many plays since retiring from the legal profession in 1992. His translations have also appeared on Project Gutenberg, the Alexandre Dumas Père web page, Literature in the Age of Napoléon, Infinite Artistries. com, and Munsey's (formerly Blackmask). In 2006 he received an award from the North American Jules Verne Society for his translations of Verne's plays. He lives and works in México.